Massachusetts Ecoregions

- ☐ Northeastern Highlands
- ▨ Northeastern Coastal Zone
- ☐ Atlantic Coastal Pine Barrens

1. Pleasant Valley Wildlife Sanctuary
2. Great Falls Discovery Center
3. Boston Nature Center & Wildlife Sanctuary
4. Arcadia Wildlife Sanctuary
5. Norcross Wildlife Sanctuary
6. Broad Meadow Brook Conservation Center & Wildlife Sanctuary
7. Oxbow National Wildlife Refuge (NWR)
8. Great Meadows NWR
9. Broadmoor Wildlife Sanctuary
10. Assabet River NWR
11. Habitat Education Center & Wildlife Sanctuary
12. Joppa Flats Education Center
13. Parker River NWR
14. Boston Nature Center
15. Blue Hills Trailside Museum
16. North River Wildlife Sanctuary
17. Cape Cod National Seashore
18. Wellfleet Bay Wildlife Sanctuary
19. Monomoy NWR
20. Nantucket NWR
21. Green Briar Nature Center
22. Mashpee NWR
23. Felix Neck Wildlife Sanctuary
24. Harvard Museum of Natural History
25. Cape Cod Museum of Natural History
26. Berkshire Museum
27. EcoTarium

Waterford Press publishes reference guides that introduce readers to nature observation, outdoor recreation and survival skills. Product information is featured on the website: www.waterfordpress.com.

Text & illustrations © 2011, 2022 Waterford Press Inc. All rights reserved. Photos © Shutterstock. Ecoregion map © The National Atlas of the United States. To order or for information on custom published products please call 800-434-2555 or email orderdesk@waterfordpress.com. For permissions or to share comments email editor@waterfordpress.com.

Made in the USA

ISBN 978-1-58355-629-0 $7.95 U.S.

50795

9 781583 556290

T0123993

8 84682 01026 3

2208915

10 9 8 7 6 5 4 3 2 1

MASSACHUSETTS WILDLIFE

MASSACHUSETTS WILDLIFE – A Folding Pocket Guide to Familiar Animals

Kavanagh/Leung

A Folding Pocket Guide to Familiar Animals

Spiny Sun Star
Crossaster papposus
To 14 in. (35 cm)

Green Sea Urchin
Strongylocentrotus droebachiensis
To 3 in. (8 cm)

Blood Star
Henricia sanguinolenta
To 4 in. (10 cm)

Sand Dollar
Echinarachnius parma
To 3 in. (8 cm)
Skeletons, called 'tests', often wash up on beaches.

Horseshoe Crab
Limulus polyphemus
To 12 in. (30 cm) wide.

Common Sea Star
Asterias forbesi
To 10 in. (25 cm)
May be tan, brown, orange or olive with orange highlights.

Blue Mussel
Mytilus edulis
To 4 in. (10 cm)
Grows attached to pilings and other marine objects.

Atlantic Bay Scallop
Argopecten irradians
To 3 in. (8 cm)

New England Neptune
Neptunea lyrata decemcostata
To 5 in. (13 cm)
Massachusetts' state shell.

Eastern Oyster
Crassostrea virginica
To 10 in. (25 cm)

Northern Quahog
Mercenaria mercenaria
To 5 in. (13 cm)
Found in mud near low tide mark.

Soft-shelled Clam
Mya arenaria
To 6 in. (15 cm)

Blue Crab
Callinectes sapidus
To 9 in. (23 cm)

Knobbed Whelk
Busycon carica
To 9 in. (23 cm)
Note prominent knobs on spire.

Hermit Crab
Pagurus spp.
To 1.3 in. (3.6 cm)
Lives in discarded shells.

Green Crab
Carcinus maenas
To 3 in. (8 cm)

Seven-spotted Lady Bug
Coccinella septempunctata
To .25 in. (.6 cm)
Massachusetts' state insect.

Praying Mantis
Family Mantidae
To 2.5 in. (6 cm)
Front legs are held as if praying.

Wood Tick
Dermacentor spp.
To .25 in. (.6 cm)
Feeds on blood and drops off when full. Can transmit diseases.

Black-and-yellow Garden Spider
Argiope aurantia
To 1.25 in. (3.2 cm)

Monarch
Danaus plexippus
To 4 in. (10 cm)

Ebony Jewelwing
Calopteryx maculata
To 1.75 in. (4.5 cm)
Like most damselflies, it rests with its wings held together over its back.

Green Darner
Anax junius
To 3 in. (8 cm)
Has a bright green thorax and a blue body. Like most dragonflies, it rests with its wings open.

Viceroy
Limenitis archippus
To 3 in. (8 cm)
Told from similar monarch by its smaller size and the thin, black band on its hindwings.

Red-spotted Purple
Limenitis arthemis astyanax
To 3.5 in. (9 cm)

Mourning Cloak
Nymphalis antiopa
To 3.5 in. (9 cm)

Eastern Tiger Swallowtail
Papilio glaucus
To 6 in. (15 cm)

Cecropia Silkmoth
Hyalophora cecropia
To 6 in. (15 cm)

Luna Moth
Actias luna
To 4.5 in. (11 cm)

Polyphemus Moth
Antheraea polyphemus
To 6 in. (15 cm)

Eastern Tiger Swallowtail Caterpillar

Monarch Caterpillar

Rainbow Trout
Oncorhynchus mykiss To 44 in. (1.1 m)
Note reddish side stripe.

Atlantic Salmon
Salmo salar To 4.5 ft. (1.4 m)
Silvery fish has spots (often X-shaped) on sides but not on fins. Freshwater version is brown-bronze colored and called landlocked salmon.

Pumpkinseed
Lepomis gibbosus
To 16 in. (40 cm)
Green-orange fish has red-black spot on ear flap.

Black Crappie
Pomoxis spp.
To 16 in. (40 cm)
Note humped back.

Bluegill
Lepomis macrochirus
To 16 in. (40 cm)

American Shad
Alosa sapidissima
To 30 in. (75 cm)
Note line of spots behind gill cover.

Striped Bass
Morone saxatilis To 6 ft. (1.8 m)
Has 6-9 dark side stripes.

Largemouth Bass
Micropterus salmoides To 40 in. (1 m)
Note prominent stripe down side, jaw extends past eye.

Smallmouth Bass
Micropterus dolomieu To 27 in. (68 cm)
Jaw joint is beneath the eye.

Bluefish
Pomatomus saltatrix To 43 in. (1.1 m)
Short first dorsal fin has 7-8 spines.

Yellow Perch
Perca flavescens To 16 in. (40 cm)
Note 6-9 dark 'saddles' down its side.

Spiny Dogfish
Squalus acanthias To 5 ft. (1.5 m)

Atlantic Cod
Gadus morhua To 4 ft. (1.2 m)
Fleshy fish has single barbel.
Massachusetts' state fish.

Flounder
Paralichthys spp. To 3 ft. (90 cm)

Yellow-Spotted Salamander
Ambystoma maculatum
To 10 in. (25 cm)

Red Eft
Notophthalmus viridescens To 6 in. (15 cm)
Juvenile form of a red-spotted newt.

Green Frog
Lithobates clamitans
To 4 in. (10 cm)
Single-note call is a banjo-like twang.

American Toad
Anaxyrus americanus
To 4.5 in. (11 cm)
Call is a high musical trill lasting up to 30 seconds.

Bullfrog
Lithobates catesbeianus
To 8 in. (20 cm)
Call is a deep-pitched – jug-o-rum.

Spring Peeper
Pseudacris crucifer
To 1.5 in. (4 cm)
Note clark X on back. Musical call is a series of short peeps.

Brown Snake
Storeria dekayi To 20 in. (50 cm)
Has 2 rows of dark spots down its back.

Smooth Green Snake
Opheodrys vernalis
To 26 in. (65 cm)

Eastern Box Turtle
Terrapene carolina
To 9 in. (23 cm)
Note high-domed shell.

Ringneck Snake
Diadophis punctatus
To 30 in. (75 cm)

Northern Water Snake
Nerodia sipedon To 4.5 ft. (1.4 m)
Note dark blotches on back.

Eastern Painted Turtle
Chrysemys picta To 10 in. (25 cm)
Note red marks on outer edge of shell.

Milk Snake
Lampropeltis triangulum To 7 ft. (2.1 m)

Snapping Turtle
Chelydra serpentina
To 18 in. (45 cm)
Note knobby shell and long tail.

Common Garter Snake
Thamnophis spp. To 4 ft. (1.2 m)
Color and pattern are variable. Has a yellowish back stripe.
Massachusetts' state reptile.

Copperhead
Agkistrodon contortrix To 52 in. (1.3 m)
Venomous snake has hourglass-shaped bands down its back.

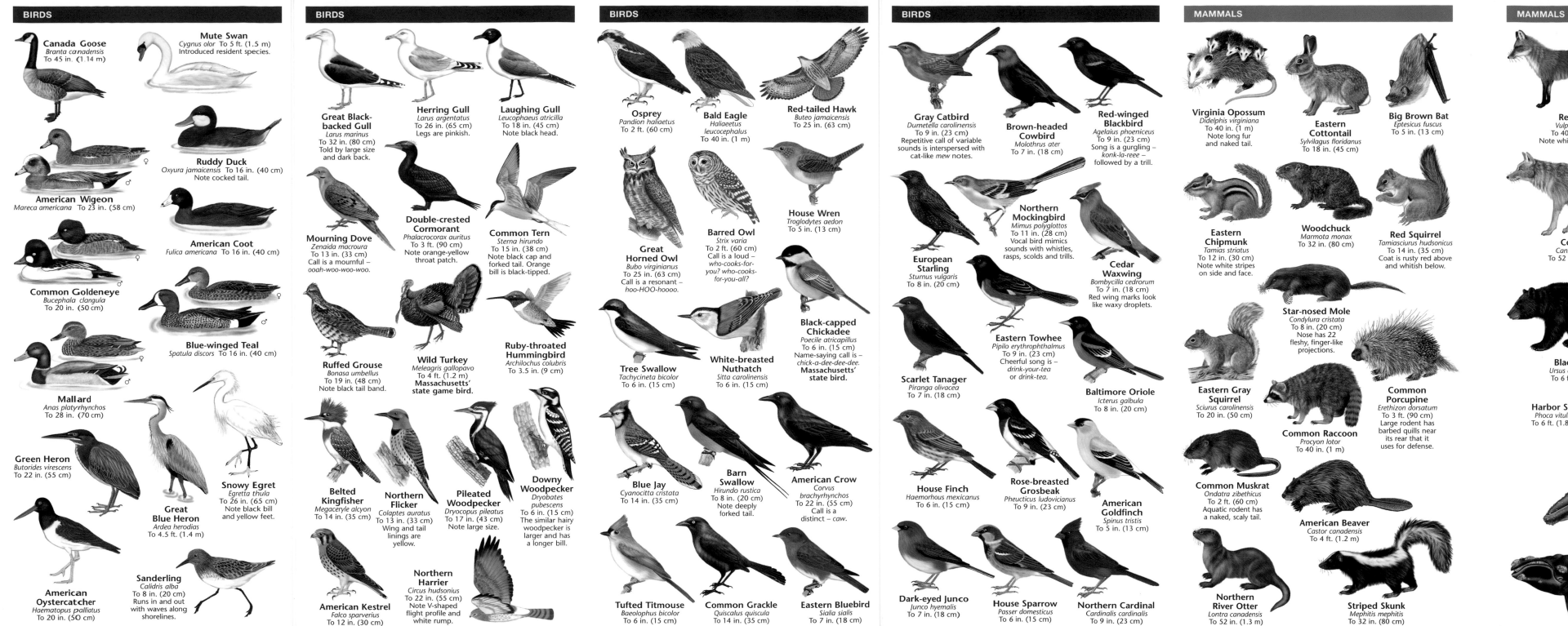

Canada Goose
Branta canadensis
To 45 in. (1.14 m)

Mute Swan
Cygnus olor To 5 ft. (1.5 m)
Introduced resident species.

Ruddy Duck
Oxyura jamaicensis To 16 in. (40 cm)
Note cocked tail.

American Wigeon
Mareca americana To 23 in. (58 cm)

American Coot
Fulica americana To 16 in. (40 cm)

Common Goldeneye
Bucephala clangula
To 20 in. (50 cm)

Blue-winged Teal
Spatula discors To 16 in. (40 cm)

Mallard
Anas platyrhynchos
To 28 in. (70 cm)

Green Heron
Butorides virescens
To 22 in. (55 cm)

Snowy Egret
Egretta thula
To 24 in. (60 cm)
Note black bill
and yellow feet.

Great Blue Heron
Ardea herodias
To 4.5 ft. (1.4 m)

American Oystercatcher
Haematopus palliatus
To 20 in. (50 cm)

Sanderling
Calidris alba
To 8 in. (20 cm)
Runs in and out
with waves along
shorelines.

Great Black-backed Gull
Larus marinus
To 32 in. (80 cm)
Told by large size
and dark back.

Herring Gull
Larus argentatus
To 26 in. (65 cm)
Legs are pinkish.

Laughing Gull
Leucophaeus atricilla
To 18 in. (45 cm)
Note black head.

Mourning Dove
Zenaida macroura
To 13 in. (33 cm)
Call is a mournful –
ooah-woo-woo-woo.

Double-crested Cormorant
Phalacrocorax auritus
To 3 ft. (90 cm)
Note orange-yellow
throat patch.

Common Tern
Sterna hirundo
To 15 in. (38 cm)
Note black cap and
forked tail. Orange
bill is black-tipped.

Ruffed Grouse
Bonasa umbellus
To 19 in. (48 cm)
Note black tail band.

Wild Turkey
Meleagris gallopavo
To 4 ft. (1.2 m)
Massachusetts'
state game bird.

Ruby-throated Hummingbird
Archilochus colubris
To 3.5 in. (9 cm)

Belted Kingfisher
Megaceryle alcyon
To 14 in. (35 cm)

Northern Flicker
Colaptes auratus
To 13 in. (33 cm)
Wing and tail
linings are
yellow.

Pileated Woodpecker
Dryocopus pileatus
To 17 in. (43 cm)
Note large size.

Downy Woodpecker
Dryobates pubescens
To 6 in. (15 cm)
The similar hairy
woodpecker is
larger and has
a longer bill.

American Kestrel
Falco sparverius
To 12 in. (30 cm)

Northern Harrier
Circus hudsonius
To 22 in. (55 cm)
Note V-shaped
flight profile and
white rump.

Osprey
Pandion haliaetus
To 2 ft. (60 cm)

Bald Eagle
Haliaeetus leucocephalus
To 40 in. (1 m)

Red-tailed Hawk
Buteo jamaicensis
To 25 in. (63 cm)

Great Horned Owl
Bubo virginianus
To 25 in. (63 cm)
Call is a resonant –
hoo-HOO-hoooo.

Barred Owl
Strix varia
To 2 ft. (60 cm)
Call is a loud –
who-cooks-for-
you? who-cooks-
for-you-all?

House Wren
Troglodytes aedon
To 5 in. (13 cm)

Black-capped Chickadee
Poecile atricapillus
To 6 in. (15 cm)
Name-saying call is –
chick-a-dee-dee-dee.
Massachusetts'
state bird.

Tree Swallow
Tachycineta bicolor
To 6 in. (15 cm)

White-breasted Nuthatch
Sitta carolinensis
To 6 in. (15 cm)

Blue Jay
Cyanocitta cristata
To 14 in. (35 cm)

Barn Swallow
Hirundo rustica
To 8 in. (20 cm)
Note deeply
forked tail.

American Crow
Corvus brachyrhynchos
To 22 in. (55 cm)
Call is a
distinct – caw.

Tufted Titmouse
Baeolophus bicolor
To 6 in. (15 cm)

Common Grackle
Quiscalus quiscula
To 14 in. (35 cm)

Eastern Bluebird
Sialia sialis
To 7 in. (18 cm)

Gray Catbird
Dumetella carolinensis
To 9 in. (23 cm)
Repetitive call of variable
sounds is interspersed with
cat-like *mew* notes.

Brown-headed Cowbird
Molothrus ater
To 7 in. (18 cm)

Red-winged Blackbird
Agelaius phoeniceus
To 9 in. (23 cm)
Song is a gurgling –
konk-la-reee –
followed by a trill.

European Starling
Sturnus vulgaris
To 8 in. (20 cm)

Northern Mockingbird
Mimus polyglottos
To 11 in. (28 cm)
Vocal bird mimics
sounds with whistles,
rasps, scolds and trills.

Cedar Waxwing
Bombycilla cedrorum
To 7 in. (18 cm)
Red wing marks look
like waxy droplets.

Scarlet Tanager
Piranga olivacea
To 7 in. (18 cm)

Eastern Towhee
Pipilo erythrophthalmus
To 9 in. (23 cm)
Cheerful song is –
drink-your-tea
or drink-tea.

Baltimore Oriole
Icterus galbula
To 8 in. (20 cm)

House Finch
Haemorhous mexicanus
To 6 in. (15 cm)

Rose-breasted Grosbeak
Pheucticus ludovicianus
To 9 in. (23 cm)

American Goldfinch
Spinus tristis
To 5 in. (13 cm)

Dark-eyed Junco
Junco hyemalis
To 7 in. (18 cm)

House Sparrow
Passer domesticus
To 6 in. (15 cm)

Northern Cardinal
Cardinalis cardinalis
To 9 in. (23 cm)

Virginia Opossum
Didelphis virginiana
To 40 in. (1 m)
Note long fur
and naked tail.

Eastern Cottontail
Sylvilagus floridanus
To 18 in. (45 cm)

Big Brown Bat
Eptesicus fuscus
To 5 in. (13 cm)

Eastern Chipmunk
Tamias striatus
To 12 in. (30 cm)
Note white stripes
on side and face.

Woodchuck
Marmota monax
To 32 in. (80 cm)

Red Squirrel
Tamiasciurus hudsonicus
To 14 in. (35 cm)
Coat is rusty red above
and whitish below.

Star-nosed Mole
Condylura cristata
To 8 in. (20 cm)
Nose has 22
fleshy, finger-like
projections.

Eastern Gray Squirrel
Sciurus carolinensis
To 20 in. (50 cm)

Common Porcupine
Erethizon dorsatum
To 3 ft. (90 cm)
Large rodent has
barbed quills near
its rear that it
uses for defense.

Common Raccoon
Procyon lotor
To 40 in. (1 m)

Common Muskrat
Ondatra zibethicus
To 2 ft. (60 cm)
Aquatic rodent has
a naked, scaly tail.

American Beaver
Castor canadensis
To 4 ft. (1.2 m)

Northern River Otter
Lontra canadensis
To 52 in. (1.3 m)

Striped Skunk
Mephitis mephitis
To 32 in. (80 cm)

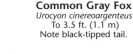

Red Fox
Vulpes vulpes
To 40 in. (1 m)
Note white-tipped tail.

Common Gray Fox
Urocyon cinereoargenteus
To 3.5 ft. (1.1 m)
Note black-tipped tail.

Coyote
Canis latrans
To 52 in. (1.3 m)

Bobcat
Lynx rufus
To 4 ft. (1.2 m)

White-tailed Deer
Odocoileus virginianus
To 7 ft. (2.1 m)
Fluffy tail is white below and
held aloft when running.

Black Bear
Ursus americanus
To 6 ft. (1.8 m)

Harbor Seal
Phoca vitulina
To 6 ft. (1.8 m)

Humpback Whale
Megaptera novaeangliae To 50 ft. (15 m)
Long flippers have scalloped edges.

Right Whale
Eubalaena glacialis To 50 ft. (15 m)
Massachusetts' state marine mammal.